The Animal Games

written by
B J Guy

Michael Terence Publishing

First published in paperback in 2022 by
Michael Terence Publishing
www.mtp.agency

ISBN 9781800942974

Copyright © 2022 B J Guy

B J Guy has asserted the right to be identified as
the author of this work in accordance with the
Copyright, Designs and Patents Act 1988

No part of this publication may be reproduced, stored in a retrieval system,
or transmitted in any form or by any means, electronic,
mechanical, photocopying, recording or otherwise,
without the prior permission of the publisher

Illustrations
Copyright © Yod67, VectorGoods
www.123rf.com

CHAPTER ONE
THE ANIMAL GAMES

The sun was just showing its face over the horizon throwing its first light of the day onto the closed eyelids of Tommy the Mouse. Slowly he started to stir, moving into his morning ritual of stretching out his legs and rubbing his eyes. Shoving his pink feet out of his warm home and blinking his eyes he began to focus on the new day in front of him and made his way over to his best friend Ronnie the Rabbit.

"Hey Ronnie, how is your training going?" Tommy asked.

"Everything's fine, Tommy," replied Ronnie, "don't forget, although I have entered for the hop, skip and jump this is a normal part of my day so I don't really need to train, apart from putting the three parts together. What about you, Tommy, have you been training for your event?"

"I can't really train for my event, Ronnie, it's called find the cheese and normally you would expect the mouse with the strongest sense of smell to win wouldn't you? Well, that may not quite be true."

"What do you mean by that, Tommy?" asked Ronnie, now getting confused. "Your event is to find a small square of cheese and you are telling me that you may not need your nose?"

"The nose part may not be as important as you think," continued Tommy. "I just hope that my plan will work for me tomorrow. Anyway, Ronnie, let's go over to Wisey."

The two friends then walked over to a large oak tree that was in the middle of their field where

Wisey, a tawny owl, lived. He was the eldest of the animals and therefore the spokesperson for the hamlet of Toddington, the home of Tommy and the rest of the gang. The animals had named their little hamlet after the larger village of Upper Toddington, a short distance away. To use part of a nearby village's name was quite common for animals and indeed Sodden, the team who had challenged Toddington to an Animal Games contest, had also taken their name from their nearby village of Lower Sodden which was about a mile from Upper Toddington.

"Listen, Wisey," said Tommy, looking up into the tree, "I know that you have accepted a challenge from Sodden to compete in the Games but do you think that we have any chance against them?"

"We have more than a chance, boys," said a voice behind Tommy. Fred the Fox was competing in the 400 metres and looking exhausted after just finishing three laps of the main field in his training programme. Gathering his breath, Fred went on, "We have one thing in common that they do not have and that is comradeship and respect for each other."

"Yes, Fred, but will that win us medals?" asked Billy the Badger, ambling up to join the conversation.

"Listen, you lot," said Wisey reassuringly, "what we don't want is a lack of belief in ourselves. Don't forget, they will be here in two hours so let's all get ready."

Immediately the commune sprang into life. Claud,

the horse, Gertie the hen, and Milly the sheep who all lived at the nearby farm had agreed to help their friends in this challenge. As Claud, who was entered in the two-laps-around-the-field event started to do his customary jogging and stepping exercises, Gertie, who had entered for the egg and spoon race, was juggling eggs to improve her balance technique. A few yards away, Billy was lifting a massive log above his head as he trained for the badger weight wrestling event.

Tommy the Mouse and Ronnie the Rabbit decided to have a walk around the sports field to try and encourage their mates. As the excitement built up, all they could hear was chirping and groaning and shouts from Wisey along the lines of, "Come on lads a bit more effort please!"

Fred was now just doing some light jogging after his earlier exertions and looking quite fit.

"You are looking good, Fred," said Tommy, "but have you heard that your opponent for the 400 metres holds the area record?"

"I have indeed, young Tommy," replied Fred, "and, if you are thinking that I haven't a chance of beating him... well, let's just say that all you can do is to give your best.

"Good luck, Fred," said Ronnie, as the two friends carried on around the field and at the same time being careful not to get in the way of Claud the horse who was running around neighing.

Suddenly, Chesty the robin who was taking his turn as the camp lookout landed on the sports field.

"They're coming lads!" Chesty shouted excitedly. "They're coming, they're coming!"

"Nice and calm everyone," said Wisey, "remember, it's taking part that counts."

As the Toddington team gathered in their show of unity, the Sodden team came into view.

"Blimey," said Tommy, "they're taking it a bit serious aren't they. There's a bit of a procession coming this way."

"Where's the music coming from, Chesty?" Wisey enquired.

"Well, there are four Ducks leading them, Wisey. they seem to be playing flutes made of reeds. It sounds like they are playing a marching song. There is also a Horse with a Woodpecker on his back."

"What's that all about, Chesty?" said Billy, putting down his log.

"Oh, their Woodpecker is tapping out a marching rhythm on a drum around the Horse's neck. Last of all there are some rabbits with vests on, all the same colour holding up a banner which reads TODDINGTON, YOUR TIME IS UP, YOU'RE HISTORY"!

"Don't panic everyone, that's what they want," said Wisey, as the Sodden team covered the last few metres and formed a line facing the Toddington team on the sports field."

"Hello, Clogsy, welcome to our home. I see that you have brought along a mighty team."

"Yes, Wisey and we are really looking forward to

competing against your team. We are very experienced in these Games events and I am surprised that you accepted our challenge. Your team could lose badly!"

The Toddington team were looking alarmed at hearing these words from Clogsy, so Wisey decided to calm his friends' nerves...

"There is no harm in losing as long as you do your best, Clogsy, and as for losing badly, well, let's just see what happens."

The two leaders had previously agreed for Willy the Toddington Woodpecker to print out an agenda of the forthcoming Games events on the oak tree in the next field which was now the main sports field. They led their armies over and the animals looked up excitedly at the list to look for their event.

THE EVENTS ARE AS FOLLOWS:
(Toddington's competitors)

DAY 1

1.00 EVENT 1
The 27 metre Marathon Speedy the Tortoise

1.45 EVENT 2
The fence jumping contest Milly the Sheep

2.30 EVENT 3
The two-lap field race Claude the Horse

3.15 EVENT 4
The javelin Chesty the Robin

4.45 EVENT 5

Intelligence and observation Wisey the Owl

5.30 EVENT 6

The underground race Moley the Mole

DAY 2

1.00 EVENT 7

The egg and spoon race Gertie the Hen

1.45 EVENT 8

Finding the cheese contest Tommy the Mouse

2.30 EVENT 9

Burying 100 nuts contest Sam the Squirrel

3.15 EVENT 10

Hop skip and jump Ronnie the Rabbit

4.00 EVENT 11

The fencing contest Willy the Woodpecker

4.45 EVENT 12

The 400 metres Fred the Fox

5.30 EVENT 13

The wrestling contest Billy the Badger

There were a few excited murmurings from the various animals about the different times when they were competing. Then a very large, rough-looking Badger with a very loud voice shouted from the back...

"I don't care who this Billy is, he is dead meat!"

And, at the same time Felix the Sodden Fox was

heard to say, "As the area record holder in the 400 metres I will have no worries about this Fred from Toddington. He will only see the back of my head!"

Wisey decided to explain to Clogsy the design of the events list.

"Clogsy, I realise that your team are very experienced, and you do not need to see your names on the events list, just the times when they are competing but I hope you understand that I needed Willy to print out our lads' names as it is our first Games and they will need a bit of guidance."

"Oh, names on trees aren't important to us, Wisey, only medals!" replied a smirking Clogsy.

The two leaders had already agreed that Wisey, as the home team leader, would have the honour of officially opening and closing the games, so Wisey hopped on to a lower branch of the oak tree and, after clearing his throat, he said in a proud voice, and, to the cheers of everyone...

"I declare that these Animal Games between Toddington and Sodden have now started!"

CHAPTER 2
LET THE GAMES BEGIN

The first event of the day was the longest. It was a marathon race between Speedy the Toddington Tortoise and his opponent from Sodden. The race was contested over 27 metres instead of the human distance of 27 miles and the Tortoise record was 4 hours and 42 minutes. As soon as this race started the rest of the Games sprung into life.

The second event involved Milly the sheep who was a little bit nervous for her fence jumping event and although all the Toddington camp were in the sports field to cheer her on, she lost to the Sodden Sheep called Mary.

Claud the Horse, was the next Toddington team member to compete but just lost in the two-lap-field-race by a few centimetres. He said that he was only beaten because of his opponent's rather large head.

By now Sodden were getting excited and shouts of, "Who do we appreciate?" and "Losers by the farmer's gate" were echoing around the field.

The Toddington team were getting really worried now and this was made worse when Chesty the Robin lost. All Robins tend to 'bob about' and Chesty was no exception to this. Apparently, he was a bit too excited in his event and couldn't resist bobbing when he was about to throw the javelin and was disqualified for stepping over the throwing line.

Chesty was very disappointed to let down his friends but they all agreed that it was just bad luck that he happened to bob at the wrong time.

Three hours had gone by very quickly for the Toddington team who were losing the Games by the score of no wins for them and three wins for Sodden.

Suddenly it was Wisey's turn as he stepped up to make it his business to raise the moral of the Toddington team. He was looking very positive as he proceeded to win the upside-down crossword against Clogsy, the Sodden leader. Clogsy then managed to win at Cluedo which then just left the chess contest to decide the winner. Clogsy then tried to put Wisey off his concentration by coughing continuously but it didn't work and a confident Wisey won the chess contest with an amazing 6 moves to the cheers of his teammates.

His opponent, Clogsy, had been given his name by the Sodden team as he had a reputation for being a bit of a clever clogs and he didn't take his defeat very well as he kept repeating to himself, "I'll beat him next time."

A smiling Wisey just replied, "Come on lads, let's show them what we can do."

The score was now 3-1 to Sodden but unfortunately for Toddington their team went further behind when Moley, their resident mole, lost his underground race to the Sodden mole.

Moley complained about the fairness of the race saying that he had lost some time after stopping to eat some worms that had been deliberately placed there by the Sodden team. Unfortunately, the panel of judges (which consisted of two animals from each camp and a guest announcer who was also a referee and came from another camp) overruled his objections and the score was now reading Sodden 4 : Toddington 1.

Suddenly everyone's attention was focussed on the remaining few centimetres of the last event of the day, the marathon, with Speedy the Toddington Tortoise leading. His opponent from Sodden was looking exhausted and was trying to hang on to his back leg but Speedy shrugged him off and, to the delight of everyone at Toddington, he crossed the finishing line first in the respectable time of 4 hours and 46 minutes.

As the evening drew in, the scoreboard was now showing Sodden 4 : Toddington 2 and while the two teams settled down in their different fields for the night, Tommy the Mouse and Ronnie the Rabbit were having a bit of a chat.

"We have done quite well on the first day against a good team, haven't we, Tommy?"

"Yes, Ronnie." replied Tommy, "it was great when Wisey and Speedy both won to make the score a bit closer, but we may struggle to win the Games at the end of tomorrow."

"What do you mean, Tommy?"

"Well," went on Tommy, "Fred the Fox is running against a record holder from the Sodden team, and I cannot see us winning the wrestling event because Wisey told me that our Billy the Badger is to wrestle against an opponent who is very much bigger than him and has never lost a contest."

"There's always a first time, Tommy, surely?"

"The first time hasn't come along in 15 years, Ronnie," continued Tommy, "and most of his opponents do not last one round! This badger's name, Ronnie, is Ivan."

"What! Is that the rough-looking badger who was shouting yesterday? I didn't know that he was the famous Ivan who everyone talks about. Although I have heard of him, I have never seen him before. Apparently, all of his previous opponents have now retired."

"Why is that, Ronnie, are they now too old to wrestle?"

"No, Tommy, they still remember the soreness and

limping after wrestling him!"

"It looks like Billy hasn't a chance, Ronnie. Let's get to bed as we both have a busy day tomorrow. See you in the morning."

The two friends retired to their warm little beds under the hedgerow in the corner of their field. While Ronnie was soon asleep, Tommy wasn't finding it so easy.

"We could lose badly tomorrow," he said to himself. "How can Fred the Fox outrun his opponent from Sodden who holds the area 400 metres record and what about Billy the Badger? He could get hurt against Ivan. I just hope my plan works in the find the cheese contest."

Tommy managed to shut out his fears and decided

to think of Milly the Sheep jumping over fences and then, slowly drifted off to sleep.

CHAPTER 3
THE FINAL DAY

Tommy woke the following morning to the sound of the Sodden team going through their training routine. The Toddington team were still wondering just what they had got themselves into.

Suddenly, Billy noticed that his opponent in the wrestling event was having a massage by the Sodden Ducks.

"Who does think he is?" said Billy, shaking his head.

"They call him Ivan," Wisey replied to Billy.

"He is certainly a very large badger, but he looks a bit of a show-off to me." continued Billy "I heard that he was bragging yesterday, Is he any good?"

"Erm... he has never lost a wrestling contest in 15 years." joined in Ronnie. "Also, Billy, I heard he is better than ever as his opponents now struggle to last a round!"

"Excuse me," said Billy, "my legs have gone a bit wobbly... I think I need to sit down."

"Don't worry, Billy, I have an idea," said Wisey reassuringly. "As the wrestling is the last of the day's events, you still have some time remaining to train and this is very important as you need to concentrate on your speed!"

"You will need a bit more than speed, Billy boy," came a voice from the Sodden area as Ivan now joined in the conversation.

"Billy will handle you!" shouted Chesty.

"We can't wait for you to fall!" shouted Tommy.

"I am really looking forward to meeting your Billy

in a few hours!" said Ivan, his eyes now bulging to match his temper. "I hope that you lot have got him insured against personal injury, ha, ha! He is going to wish that he had never volunteered to compete in the wrestling event! Have you lot got plenty of rubbing ointment for his sore limbs? Ha, ha!"

Wisey, noticing that Billy was starting to look a little worried, decided to take him away from any intimidation by Ivan.

"Come on, Billy, let's go over to our training ground. We still have a few hours to work on your speed and I've also added a game to your training programme."

As Wisey led Billy to the training ground, the two companions, Tommy and Ronnie decided to join up with some of the team and support Gertie the Hen in the first event of the day, the egg and spoon race.

Gertie did not disappoint her friends and to their cheers finished first over the line making the scoreboard Sodden 4 : Toddington 3.

The next event was the one Tommy had been entered for. It consisted of lumps of cheese being buried together in a bag a few hours before by Wisey and Clogsy, the two leaders of the animal kingdoms and they had chosen quite a large area in the corner of the sports field to bury them. The rules where that the first mouse to find this bag with the lumps of cheese in was the winner.

The mouse from Sodden started running around

frantically using his nose to try and smell the buried cheese but all Tommy did was walk around looking at the soil and then, after just a few minutes he dug down into it and pulled up the cheese.

Tommy's mates were gobsmacked as Tommy stood there with a satisfied smile on his face.

"I know that you said you had a plan, Tommy, but I cannot work out what it was," said a bemused Ronnie.

"It was easy really, Ronnie. You see, I realised that when something is buried the soil is disturbed and all I did was look for signs of that!"

The score was now showing Toddington 4 : Sodden 4 and the home camp were getting quite confident until news came in that Sam the Squirrel had lost his contest which consisted of burying 100 nuts in the shortest time. Some of the Toddington supporters said that Sam was too busy trying to remember where he had buried the nuts for future reference.

The score was now Toddington 4 : Sodden 5 and Toddington were behind once more. Ronnie's event, which was the hop, skip and jump, was next.

Chapter 4
THE EXCITEMENT BUILDS UP

The first to jump was the Sodden Rabbit who made a very good effort, and a line was drawn by the starter to show where he had jumped to.

"Be calm, Ronnie.," said Tommy, "do you want me to massage your rear legs?"

"No, Tommy, my legs are fine, and you don't need to worry about me being worried, just watch me!"

Ronnie winked at Tommy confidently as he stood on the start line and then performed an amazing hop, skip and jump to go past the line where the Sodden Rabbit had reached and win the contest.

"What a jump, Ronnie," shouted Tommy. "How come you were so confident?"

"Oh, I looked at the Sodden Rabbit and noticed that his back legs were not as long as mine and although he jumped well, I knew that I would have more spring and it proved that I was right!"

All the animals from both camps were now getting excited as the last events were unfolding and the 'oohs', and 'aahs' could be heard all around the sports field and with the score now of Toddington 5 : Sodden 5..

The Sodden team spirit was lifted once more when their Woodpecker beat Willy, the Toddington Woodpecker in the fencing contest although, to be fair to Willy his supporters said that they had never seen a beak on a Woodpecker as long as his opponents and Willy just couldn't get near him.

The Toddington team looked up at the scoreboard and the score was now showing Toddington 5 :

Sodden 6 and there were just two events to go.

"We have had a good two days competing against Sodden, Ronnie, but we are really up against it now."

"I know, Tommy. Fred is about to run against Felix, the Sodden Fox who holds the area record and after that, our Billy is facing that bully, Ivan from Sodden who has never lost a contest. So it looks like we have no chance to win these Games.

"I agree, Ronnie, but as Wisey said, 'you can have no complaints if you compete as well as you can and that is something, we can all be proud of'."

It had been an amazing two days for the animals of both camps as the Games swung from one team to the other and now everyone was excitedly waiting for the last two events to decide who were the Animal Games champions.

"Well, Tommy, although we are probably going to lose, we can still support our friends, Fred and Billy. So, let's join up with the rest of Toddington and go and watch Fred in his 400 metres race."

The two mates walked over to the running track where everyone else had gathered and Fred was looking surprisingly relaxed as he crouched down on the starting line alongside Felix.

"You've no chance, Freddie," said Felix. "I hold the record for this distance."

"Sometimes in life, Felix... the unexpected can happen," replied Fred with a confident smile on his face.

Suddenly, the excited crowd of animals from both camps went quiet as they heard the announcer say... "Get ready boys... go!"

To the surprise of everyone, especially the Toddington team, Fred shot out from the start line and didn't ease up until he reached the finishing line, leaving Felix well behind.

As his friends were rejoicing the announcer could be heard saying, "The winner of the 400 metres in a new area record time of 32.7 seconds is Fred from Toddington." And a completely exhausted Felix who could hardly speak just said... "How?"

Fred walked away smiling and after further questions from very happy teammates said, "All right, none of you know this but my dad was a very good runner who once held the national record for the 400 metres and when I was growing up he always encouraged me to follow in his footsteps and said that I could be as fast as him... if I trained properly."

"Well, you all know me. I would much prefer to enjoy the afternoon sun than train as it seemed like too much hard work, but this time was different. When Wisey announced that he had agreed to a sports challenge from the Sodden camp and asked me to run for Toddington, I was so proud that I decided to train just like my dad told me to and I couldn't believe how much my speed improved as a result. The rest, as they say my friends... is history!"

As the rejoicing team drifted away to the last

event, Fred made his way to a little corner of the sports field and said... "This win was for you as well as Toddington, Dad. I know that you are watching from somewhere and I hope that I have made you proud."

Meanwhile, Clogsy, the leader of the Sodden team, sought out Wisey to have a chat.

"Your team have done quite well so far, Wisey, against us, but this is where your success will end. I know that the score is now six all and the next event will decide who are the local Animal Games champions, but I am afraid that this is where your luck will run out... Ivan will see to that!"

"He may well do, Clogsy, but life can be strange sometimes."

"Your Badger hasn't a chance against ours, just look at the difference in size!"

"Sometimes brain power can outlast brawn power, Clogsy."

"Wisey, the only way your Badgers brain can help is to tell him to jump out of the ring and run as fast as he can!"

"We shall see, my dear Clogsy..." replied Wisey. "We shall see."

Chapter 5
THE FINAL EVENT

The sound of trumpets filled the air as the Sodden Ducks changed from their reed flutes to play massive Lilies and then the announcer said the words... "We now arrive at the final event of this Games with the scores level at Toddington 6 : Sodden 6. We shall now commence with the Badger weight wrestling contest between Ivan, from Sodden and Billy, from Toddington."

A hush settled over the daisy-chain ring as Ivan entered, jogging around and raising his arms in the air to cheers from the Sodden supporters. Looking over with wild eyes to the opposite side where Billy was, he then started flexing his muscles and shouted, "There's no escape for you now boy!"

"He sure looks fearsome, Ronnie," whispered

Tommy, "look at the size of his paws!"

The two friends glanced around at both sets of supporters and noticed Gertie, now looking alarmed alongside them with her hands over her eyes... unable to look because of what may happen to Billy.

In Billy's corner, Wisey was massaging his legs and said, "Right then, Billy, take no notice of what he is doing, he is just trying to frighten you. For the last few hours, we have been concentrating on your speed because that is what you will need for sure against Ivan but there is another thing to concentrate on and that will involve being calm. Remember when we introduced that new game in your training programme when you had to avoid being touched by Milly?" She was chasing behind trying to touch you and you had to make sure that she didn't - without looking at her face, only at her feet?"

"Well, although I have only seen Ivan wrestle once, I have noticed that he could have a weakness."

"A weakness, Wisey? I can't wait to hear this!" Billy replied.

"If Ivan cannot get to grips with his opponent he tends to rush in blindly. His opponents seeing this, panic, and they lose the contest. Billy, this could be a chance for you, but you must remain calm. When Ivan rushes at his opponent he loses a bit of balance and clumsily gets his feet wrong. If you can stay calm and watch his feet for this then there may be a chance to slide his leading foot against his other one and if you can manage to push him at the same time he could go over." Wisey took a long breadth and carried on, "You are smaller than him, Billy, so can turn quicker and use your speed until that moment comes."

"It will never work, Wisey, how can I be that calm?"

"You could be a hero for all of Toddington today, Billy. We are all rooting for you!"

Ivan was in the opposite corner of the ring and talking to the referee. "Hey, Ref, they are doing too much talking over there. Let's get this contest started!" Ivan then shouted over to Billy, "Hey, little Billy Boy, stop talking to your bird friend and come into the middle of the ring. I have a present for you!"

The referee walked to the centre of the daisy-chain ring and called the two opponents over to him. "Right gentlemen, I want this to be a fair contest with no biting or scratching. This is a wrestling match, and these are the rules that you will follow. There will be three rounds of two minutes each round and the first badger to fall loses. Do you both understand?"

"Let's get started, Ref, and I'll make sure this little weasel understands," growled Ivan.

Billy had a quick look around and noticed that Gertie still had her hands over her eyes and at the same time heard a voice from the Sodden Horse saying, "I will bet anyone a bundle of hay that Billy doesn't last 20 seconds!"

Everywhere that Billy looked he could see the worried faces of his Toddington mates but he decided to stand up to Ivan and shouted... "Words don't win contests, big head," to the cheers from his watching friends.

An old, discarded bicycle bell was rung by one of the ducks to start the first round which began with Ivan rushing over to Billy, an eerie smile on his face as he attempted to grab him, only to find that he was not there. He then continued to chase Billy around the ring for the next minute.

"Stay still your slippery eel," whispered Ivan as he managed to get a bit closer to Billy. "Let me massage your limbs for you."

"No chance big mouth," replied Billy as he danced

away once more, "you couldn't catch a cold with your pace."

Billy was surprising himself at how he was standing up to a badger who was a lot bigger than him but suddenly, Ivan guessed the way that Billy was turning, and the two fighters locked paws. Billy could feel the enormous power of Ivan and gasped as he tried to hold his ground.

"I'm going to make you suffer first before I flatten you six feet under!" said Ivan, his eyes bulging and, grabbing Billy around the waist, he started to squeeze.

Billy looked over to Wisey who said, "Spin him, Billy, use your speed!"

Quickly gathering his breadth, Billy trod on Ivan's

feet and spun out of his grip to the shouts of "Foul!" from Ivan's supporters.

The referee shouted, "Fight on you two!" and as Ivan chased Billy across the ring all he could catch was air as Billy, using his speed slipped under his paws and, after tapping Ivan on the back of his head retreated into the centre of the ring.

Suddenly, as an enraged Ivan came after Billy, the bell sounded for the end of the first round.

Wisey was waiting for Billy in his corner with a smile on his face. "Well done, Billy, you are frustrating him, and he is losing his temper. Bullies don't like it if they can't have their own way."

"I still can't see a way to avoid him for another two rounds, Wisey."

"Trust in yourself, Billy, and try to stay calm, whatever he threatens."

The bell sounded for the second round and, as before, Ivan came rushing over to find that Billy had slipped under his paws, tapped him on his head and moved away. Ivan looked over to Billy and menacingly shouted... "You cannot run forever, boy. I am going to catch you very soon and when I do I'm going to turn your ears back to front. I'll rearrange your stripes. Come here you little rat!"

The rest of the round was very much the same as the first one with Ivan trying to catch Billy and then, with half a minute of the round left, he was successful as he at last managed to cut off Billy's escape route and grabbed him in a bear hug.

Billy could feel Ivan's hot breath in his face as he whispered, "At last Billy boy, I am going to massage your limbs as I promised." And immediately started to twist Billy's arm around his back.

Billy could feel his arm going numb with the pain and was thinking that there was no escape but suddenly the bell sounded for the end of the second round.

As Billy slowly walked back to his corner, Wisey noticed that he was getting tired and decided to try and lift his confidence.

"Well done, Billy, you are doing fantastic."

"It's a good job that the bell sounded at that moment, Wisey. I was finding it difficult to get away and was fearing for the worst. I am wondering if it is worth me going out for the last round as I haven't got much energy left and my arm is quite painful."

"Billy, we have to work hard to realise our ambitions. Just like you must now. At some time in everyone's life they will have to face a problem and dig deep to confront something. That something could range from injuries to their health, to even bullying and if they can stand up to this battle then they will learn something about themselves."

"Billy, Ivan has won before because he has frightened his opponents into defeat. If you can be calm and stand up to him for one more round, then you could forever be remembered for your bravery and you could also be remembered in folklore as the Badger who refused to be bullied!"

"Wisey, I'm going after him, let's go!"

"I'm proud of you, Billy. Just remember that if you stick to our plan, it is still possible to beat this bully but keep moving away from him until he gets frustrated and then there could be a good chance for you."

"The bell sounded for the start of the last round and a huge roar came from the two sets of supporters but, for different reasons. While the Sodden camp was roaring for Ivan to finish off Billy the Toddington camp was just hoping that he could survive without getting hurt too much.

As Ivan came rushing over, a now more determined Billy calmly ducked under his massive paws and after tapping him on his nose danced away once more.

"Stay still you little flea!" shouted Ivan yet again, frustration now showing on his face.

"You're too slow, ugly," Billy replied. "I only have to last one round and this contest will be declared a draw. Then your record of invincibility will be over, and no one will be frightened of you anymore."

Ivan was getting mad at this suggestion by Billy and was roaring and chasing him all around the ring.

Watching their friend trying to survive, Ronnie said to Tommy in an alarmed voice that he was sure he could see steam coming out of Ivan's ears and nose.

The Sodden team were all screaming for Ivan to

cut Billy off and they were rewarded as he again guessed which way Billy would turn and, twisting to one side grabbed his numb arm.. "Got you, weasel," he whispered, that eerie smile returning to his face. "Now let's get this over!"

At that moment Billy could hear Wisey shouting, "NOW, BILLY, NOW!" and, looking down, he noticed that Wisey's legs were pointing away from each other and he was unbalanced. Forgetting about the pain in his arm he quickly managed to push Ivan's other front foot alongside his lead one and, at the same time using all his strength, grabbed him and pulled.

To everyone watching it was slow motion as Ivan started to sway and then, like a giant tree, crashed to the ground, his legs in the air, with an almighty thud.

There was complete silence as the Sodden supporters could not believe what they had seen.

The same could be said for the Toddington supporters who by now were running around clacking, tweeting, howling and cheering... and telling Gertie to remove her hands from her eyes as a miracle had happened. Meanwhile, Tommy and Ronnie were hugging each other...

"I cannot believe what I have just seen, Ronnie."

"There is a saying, Tommy, 'truth is stranger than fiction'!"

"Then... I now believe in sayings, Ronnie."

A smiling Wisey was saying to himself, "I didn't really

think that Billy had much of a chance, but this proves that there is a message here about believing in yourself, and you might be surprised at what you can achieve."

As the Referee was holding one of Billy's arms up and announcing, "The winner and new Animal Games champion is Billy from Toddington!" a clearly happy and proud Wisey entered the centre of the wrestling ring...

"I declare that these Games are now over - until the next ones in 4 years' time."

He then glanced at the scoreboard which was now showing Toddington 7 : Sodden 6 and with a broad smile on his face said...

"Tell me, young Tommy. Is the result that I am

looking at real or are my eyes deceiving me?"

"Believe me, Wisey, that is a real result," replied an equally happy Tommy.

There were handshakes all around, apart from a still shocked Ivan who was threatening to beat Billy easily next time to a reply from Billy of...

"You will be even slower next time, bully boy!"

To further cheering from Toddington, the Sodden team made their way home behind their ducks who were now playing 'we shall overcome'.

CHAPTER 6
ANYONE FOR HAY?

As the Sodden team disappeared into the distance, Billy, everyone's hero, was being carried around the home camp on the back of Claud, the Toddington horse, to the delight of their mates.

Wisey quickly arranged a small party for everyone, and the food was provided by the various animals.

Tommy and Ronnie made a short journey to the nearby farmers field and returned with carrots, potatoes, and swedes and Moley offered to provide some worms, which no one really fancied but it was a nice gesture by him.

The music was provided by the resident rooks who had borrowed the idea of playing reed flutes from the Sodden team and were all sitting in the oak tree playing various tunes including a barn dance for Gertie who, along with the other farm animals, Claud and Milly, had decided to stay with their mates overnight and go back to their farm tomorrow.

The party went on well into the evening with the animals remembering the events over the last two days.

"My word, it was a very close contest, eh Ronnie?"

"It sure was, Tommy," replied Ronnie, munching a carrot. "To be honest, I thought that we had lost the games a number of times."

"That is what life is about, young Ronnie," joined in Claud. "Anyone for hay? I accepted the bet from the Sodden horse and have some spare."

"We'll err... have some later, Claud," replied a very proud looking Fred.

"You were brilliant in your race, Fred," said Speedy, busily munching through his second swede. "Was your time as fast as mine?"

"Fred's time is a new area record, Speedy." said Sam the Squirrel to smiles from his mates. "Although, you did great to hold off the Sodden tortoise in the last few metres, anyone fancy a few nuts?"

Wisey, who had watched the fun with amusement was still trying to understand quite how they had all responded to his words of camp unity and had a few words left to say to them...

"I hope you have all had a good last few days, lads,"

he said. "I know that you are all enjoying the fruits of your efforts and that is a joy to see but there is one last important message that I would like to say to you. Winning is a lovely feeling and to be enjoyed but equally important is the taking part and doing the best that you can."

"Of course, you cannot win all of the time, as Ivan has now found out."

"He sure has, Wisey," interrupted Gertie to laughter from the rest of the camp.

"It is just as important," went on Wisey, "to accept losing, when that may happen and to congratulate the opposition, as the Sodden team congratulated us... apart from Ivan, but, who knows, he may be a nice Badger one day."

"I wouldn't bet my hay on that happening, Wisey," joined in Claud. "By the way... I have some left if anyone is still hungry."

The camp settled down for the night, occasionally a sleepy voice could be heard from the animals...

Ronnie... "Did anyone see my hop, skip and jump?"

Fred... "It was just another day for me... anyone want my autograph?"

Gertie... "Anyone fancy an egg and spoon race tomorrow?"

Gradually the noise from their mates got quieter and quieter leaving just Ronnie and Tommy awake.

"Do you know, Tommy, it is quite surprising what you can do when you put your mind to it."

"Yes, Ronnie, it is a lesson for us all to remember."

"Until the next time eh, Tommy?"

"Until the next time... Ronnie."

Later, when all was quiet, and the gang were asleep, Wisey asked Willy the Woodpecker to print this poem on the oak tree.

He called it:

HAVING FUN

"I've just had a thought,"
said the Mouse to the Shrew.
"We could enter a team of our own."
"That's all very well," said the Owl, looking down,
"but the Tortoise is likely to moan."

"Hold on!" said a voice from the Tortoise below
as his head popped out of his shell,
"I could enter the marathon,
    now that would be good,
when I give the stragglers hell."

"Can I enter for the hop, skip, and jump?"
said the Rabbit as he played in the morning sun,
"I'm not being vain, but I'd never need to train,
I could win this event for fun."

"Any formation events?" asked the Starlings
as they danced in the sky above.
"Or even wrestling," said the Badger,
    in his waistcoat of stripes,
"All they need is a bit of a shove."

"Are there any sleeping events?"
    asked the Hamster,
opening his eyes at the noise
"You could stand on that box if you won," replied the Owl,
"but we'd have to wake you to
    present you your prize."

"Will you permit me to say," said the Horse,
    chewing hay,
"no Human is faster than me."

"Can I run my race twice, now that would be fun
and finish with a nice cup of tea?"

"Any bobbin events?" asked the Robin looking on,
as he proudly stuck out his chest.
I already have the colours of St George,
do you think I'll still need a vest?"

"I can perform the parallel bars," said the Crow,
as he sat on the telephone line.
"And my misses can perform the floor event,
but it's not quite as good as mine."

"Hold on a bit, boys," said the Mouse once again.
"The Humans don't like to lose."
"We'll, let them win a few at first,"
    said the Magpie, joining in,
"but they may have to compete in twos."

Suddenly a voice from above said,
"I was just passing and couldn't help
    but hear all the fuss,
Can I suggest," said Mr Jay,
    "that my idea for today is,
it's not about them and us."

"Then, what's your idea, my dear?" said the Horse,
as he looked up an answered his friend.
"It's a day to ourselves," said the Jay, once again,
"a day that will never end."

And so, it happened,
    that the Animal Games was born
and the nation was spared the disgrace,
of losing to Robin and Rabbit and all
then saying, "It's not a fair race!"

So, if you're lucky enough
    to be up with the Larks,
in the rural retreat of the gang,
then notice a sign saying admission 10 pence,
    and you hear a bit of a bang,
don't be startled look on,
    at the start of their games
as they joyfully hop, skip and run,
and remember that day
    for the rest of your life

    ...it's our Animals just having fun!

The End

Available worldwide from
Amazon and all good bookstores

----

www.mtp.agency

www.facebook.com/mtp.agency

@mtp_agency

www.ingramcontent.com/pod-product-compliance
Lightning Source LLC
LaVergne TN
LVHW081544060526
838200LV00048B/2208